The Crow Road from Eden

Tony Howson was born in Slough, 1956, and spent his formative years in Yorkshire and Teesside. He has worked widely as a journalist in both print and radio, and in 2011 was awarded an Honorary Doctorate in Journalism from Uzhgorod University, Ukraine. His poetry has been widely anthologised, and his prose has appeared in a diverse variety of outlets from the *Northampton Mercury and Herald* to *The Guardian*.

He presently works for BBC Media Action, living a uniquely international existence between Kyiv, Scarborough and Dar es Salaam, Tanzania. He is married with three sons and a granddaughter. *The Crow Road from Eden* is the first published collection of his writing.

The Crow Road from Eden

TONY HOWSON

VALLEY

First published 2012 by Valley Press
Woodend, The Crescent, Scarborough, YO11 2PW
www.valleypressuk.com

ISBN: 978 1 908853 09 7
Cat. no. VP0026

9 8 7 6 5 4 3 2 1

A CIP record for this book is
available from the British Library

Printed and bound in Great Britain by
Imprint Digital, Upton Pyne, Exeter

www.valleypressuk.com/authors/tonyhowson

*This book is dedicated
to my wife, Vica*

Acknowledgements

Special thanks go to Rita and Bill Sherriff-Hammond, Beranice and Philip Semp, Nick Adcock, Russell Peasgood, Pete Everest, Diane Chandler and all at Valley Press for the views, support and recommendations that have helped bring this collection to fruition.

Contents

Introduction

Poetry is one way to tell a story, and storytellers play a vital role as travellers navigate down their road. Geoffrey Chaucer, author of the *Canterbury Tales* (and a man who was 'no poppet to embrace' with his 'elvish' expression) testifies to this. He had the character a storyteller needs to tell the tale, the charisma to make the traveller pause to listen. The potholes, the stumbles, the delays, the jams, the repair works, the roundabouts and the lane changes give the story meat to feast on. The road is not always clear. In poetry, sometimes you need patience to delve a little deeper, unravel the map of the poem and try to understand its direction; to turn around and turn around again if you have missed a signpost.

Modern times, and the storyteller is now the radio and the direction set by a 'sat nav', a part of human adaptation. These technologies may help, but not resolve, all the issues that exist on the road leading from naïve paradise. To navigate we sometimes have to draw on personal resilience. The road itself can be the road to true love, the road to hell, the road to nowhere, the road to heaven. Perhaps all these tracks are not roads but lanes running along the road from the Gates of Eden. Perhaps it is less a road, more a motorway.

The poems in this book are snapshots from my years of travel since the early 1990s. Within them are hidden the smells, the colours, the senses, sights, sounds and sensualities of the environments I found myself in. They are all based on experiences, some of them a single moment, others a combination of moments pulled together. A constant traveller, a peregrine poet, I am always a guest inside someone else's culture, which means all the poems are subjective stories of observation. I feel that I am even a guest in my native culture; part of this long journey has been the discovery that I am a 'Jack of all cultures, master of none'.

Within this book, I have divided the world into earthly regions. Each section starts with a personal overview of the space and the poetry that has impacted on me. Not everyone will agree with my interpretation of places and poets, timelines and events; if this creates a discussion about poetry, then it makes the journey more entertaining and interesting.

I hold on to four precious possessions collected on my travels. They may not be physically with me all the time, but spiritually they feed me and can be found within these pages. From Africa there are two things: one is a coffee pot used by Somali camel herders as they sat during nights round a fire telling stories, chewing over life and building their own intimate community. Another is a pillow carved from wood, used by nomads for a good night's sleep under the stars. Cordial conversation, coffee and a good night sleep are life's essentials.

From Ukraine it is a garish fish sculpted from clay and painted with bright red lips. Trapped along its sides are a series of reflections of life along the riverbank. Fish, like me, steal stories. The Romans saw fish as the keepers of dreams.

From England it is a black vase with green leaf patterns, made in the 1930s by my mother's cousin. It has accompanied me all my life, used by my mother to display plastic roses, collected from Omo or Daz washing powder packets. It now sits on my mantle-piece, but never empty. Inside this pot are my memories.

I sojourned in all the places signposted in this book; perhaps I have resided in none. To share the journey further down the Crow Road from Eden, step this way...

The Crow Road from Eden: The Human Zoo

"There is no God and we are his prophets."
– Cormac McCarthy, The Road

"God is Love. God is Spirit." – John 4:24

As I step along the Crow Road from Eden
Through the Human Zoo caged in limited time
I collect my sorrows and my pleasures
And feed them to the carnivores of rhyme.

Temptations pothole the pathway
That invites us in a stumbling dance:
Partnering the mocking monkeys,
Whose swing denies the stalker's chance.

The trembling deer of desire stands
Cornered in her limited space,
Frozen, under a predator's gaze,
Submissive, with no place to race.

And the onlooker's memory lingers
With vulture-vision of open doors,
Freeing night-terrors, in bloodthirsty thrill
At nature's rule over nature still.

Curl in your panic, or stand to fight,
On the ground tilled by virtue's misleading hand
Where Thérèse of Lisieux lights the way
With the wave of an innocent, childish wand.

Cling together in mistrusting tremble,
Or, just accept the fate of the road;
Warm by the fire of no regrets
And eat the bread from seeds once sowed.

Beyond the cages of the Human Zoo
The pathway winds out of view
Until you reach the gateway through
Which you have no choice,

But pass, though the light may be warm
Or the hour grey, cold and late,
Though no traveller knows for certain:
Is this human-animal worthy of love or hate?

But beware whose light guides you
Down the winding pathway of the Human Zoo:
It may be Lightborn with his glowing poker
You ask to walk beside of you.

Or even sister of the sack, Saint Agnes,
With her dark crow visions sent,
Or Archangel Uriel's salvation hand
And his battle cry: repent, repent, repent.

Africa

Barbara refu haikosi kona (Kiswahili proverb) –
"The long road is not without a corner"

As a child, Africa was a place that grabbed and twisted my imagination. I knew nothing about its sometime dark spiritualism, outside of witch doctors in Tarzan films. Somehow I did sense magical colour, smells, and tactile nature. I had to grow up and visit to discover the vitality of a crafted pot, chair, or tool; art and religion integrated into the daily life of Africa.

In those early days, stories springing from heroic British colonialism and Edgar Rice Burroughs attracted me. Today I see it with less innocent eyes, but the sense of adventure lingers. I remember flying low in a small aircraft over the scrub-desert edging Djibouti. I immediately found myself remembering some lost description from Biggles, as I felt the plane was just hovering, going nowhere over the expanse of sameness.

"Africa is a cruel country; it takes your heart and grinds it into powdered stone – and no one minds." – Elspeth Huxley

My first trip to Africa was in the early 90s, on the border between Cote D'Ivoire and Liberia. Not an easy time or place. Here, for the first time, I saw the extent of my vulnerability, mortality and significance, when a soldier held a gun to my head and took the safety catch off.

My next trip was to Somaliland on the Horn. The civil war had ended and I thought this was a safer area than the troubled south. Here, I was close to being shot out of the skies, shot in the back or stoned by an angry mob. I remember the rolling, rattling sound on to the metal roof and the fear of a hand-grenade explosion that never came. Another occasion, and I believed I was dying from the worst case of the archaic flux I have ever experienced.

I survived. Others have not been so lucky. I could never suffer the life of middle-class England again; something in Africa had bitten me, and when the mood was right, poems were written.

Poetry plays a heartbeat role, reflecting tradition and the oral nature of African people. I have tried to follow and explore some of it. For travelers, the blessings passed on by fellow nomads are treasured.

"Now you depart, and though your way may lead
Through airless forests thick with hagar trees,
Places steeped in heat, stifling and dry,
Where breath comes hard, and no fresh breeze can reach –
Yet may God place a shield of coolest air
Between your body and the assailant sun.
And in a random scorching flame of wind
That parches the painful throat, and sears the flesh,
May God, in his compassion, let you find
The great-boughed tree that will protect and shade."

– 19th Century poem (or 'gabay') by the Somali warrior
Sayyīd Muhammad `Abd Allāh al-Hasan[1]

Horn of Africa

My hair is thick with dust blown from some arid space.
My throat is dry and thirst unquenched by brackish water.
My clothes are stiff with sweat with colours faded in strong
    sun.
My shield of cool breeze has abandoned me, tangled in the
    Hagar tree,
My dreams cannot be seen in the shimmer of heat.
My wishes cannot be granted by leaving gifts under stones.
This desert may be the devil's home, but I cannot stay,
So I leave, but long to return, to parched places and short
    shadows,
To red rust sand and rock, to find sweet water on the beach,
To walk slowly by the graveyard of unwritten histories,
Where the bones are dry and crumbled to dust,
To where there is nothing and nothing is all, for it is true:
Here once stood the gates to the Garden of Eden, I stand
Facing the illusion of Adam and Eve, there is no life without
    sin,
Where apples and shade torture temptation, and the agony
Of knowing what is forbade, to commit the crime, to suffer
    an ending
That lifts the latch that shows the way to a new mirage.

Somalia

She is a shrew untamed
In a world so scarred
By her volatile game,
A passion unhinged,
Yet a beauty framed,
Painted by red rust of
Desert; scorched, arid,
Of breast-like mountains,
Of thorn trees scarred
By the sap-cutters' knife.

She tethers nomads
Whose eyes are on fire.
She mirrors their eyes.
She drinks the heat,
Inhales the acrid smell,
Eats it with dust
From camel hooves,
Washes in the milk,
Drinks the milk,
This shrew,

She is not for taming.

Rattling Down a Corrugated Roof

In frozen time, a rattle runs
Down the corrugated roof,
Bringing dreams and visions
Flashing into the centre of the room.

We stood, breathless, waiting
For air to be sucked, for the ball
To stop rolling, unsure heartbeats:
Is this the real thing?

The mind's eye is seeing
Toyota moving, jolting,
On a rutted dry dirt track,
Cattle flicking flies with slow tails,
Camels dancing in elegant lines,
Through needle-sharp scrub,
A broken watch shattered, innards out
On a rock, sacrificing time,
Coffined in heat.
Soaked in sweat.
Eyes squinting against stinging grains,

I stand waiting.
The room is waiting.
The sound is waiting
To change.

Drinking Orange in Cote D'Ivoire

First you squeeze it,
Slice off the top,
Then you drink it dry.

She sold oranges the colour of lemons
From a red plastic bowl balanced on her head.

Her brown, outstretched arm, proffered one
To every paused passenger surrounded

By jostling children selling cobs of corn,
Bags of water, and oranges coloured lemon.

Savour the stinging, tingling on dry lips
Enjoying an orange as the bus moves on.

Lover and rapist side by side, through villages
Of straw and mud, darkened by skyscraper shadows.

The orange lover looks back to see her,
Arm outstretched, eyes with a pleading look.

The rapist kneads the orange coloured lemon,
Slices off the top and drinks it dry.

Spellbound

Stinging stones blow off a red rust desert
The deepness of blue off a flat sea
The sound that is silence echoes with spirits
The flash of a time in a world that is frozen
The blink of an eye that stirs the still air
This smouldering landscape where devils play
On the edge of God's canvas where the oil is spread thin
Amongst angled dimensions there breathes within
The amina mystery

Nigeria

What is the use of windows in the open air
Where blue-sky curtains drape the horizon
Or a breeze-blown dust lines your collar
Cakes your nose and skin and throat
Or
Fresh rain strikes and bounces off
Earth, cracked, turning it brown from red
As water and heat mix sensuous paints
In bowls of swirls, stirring the smell of green.

Democrats, oilmen and raven-haired girls
Drink cold beer, cocktails in Sheraton Iced air,
I leave through large glass doors to the bite
Of humid heat like raw wine that hits the tongue
And
The joint of the jaw stiffens with the sensation of alcohol
Its petrol bouquet coats the throat when I need water
As I sit in the stench of honking traffic, jammed,
Weaving contradiction in a single direction.

The green of Bayelsa and its muddy river flow
Through my senses, with its eddies and whirlpools
Carrying the laughter of children with swollen stomachs,
Playing beneath the leaking pipeline
Where
Uncovered women bend and plunge in their washing
As I leave them to join the road lined with sellers
And leper-beggars, bandaged and bowing with outstretched
    hands
As I wonder of the need for windows.

The Lidless Pot

With me I carry an earthenware pot,
Rough-made by rough hands.
My pot is lidless so your troubled soul
Can fly to me. I will comfort it.

Tread carefully across the Savannah,
For the grass is tall and danger hidden.
The ripple that stirs the stillness
Can be death. Whose? Maybe yours.

Who is the stalker? Who stalks who?
Do they stalk each other? These two,
Circle walkers who, like love predators,
Have sharpened teeth for passionless kill.

Lose, and your spirit will fly
To my earthenware pot; it waits lidless
To store the soul from your crusted shell
And nurture it in a new space to fill.

Unseen empathies weave unseen paths,
Spraying the meeting points, resting
At the watering holes where enemies meet
On common ground, to stoop and drink.

When that flustered heartbeat of panic rushes,
When the stampede comes at the lion's leap,
I will be the elephant that stands before you;
But if I am not there, my pot waits, lidless.

The Cardinal's Car

for Katendi

She looked into the silvery light and said:
'I want to see my grandmother.'
Oh how she would like to ride there
In the car we believe is being used,
Throne-like litterish,
By the Congolese Cardinal.

Her grandmother lives in a village,
A long way away, in a wet forest.
Long after the road ends, bump and
Ride on dip and churn of track, plough
Through the sudden shriek of sounds,
Nostrils led by damp earth smells.

Imagine the look on the elderly faces,
In the eyes of children, on the talking women,
Imagine, seeing their village daughter
Princess descending from the high door,
Superstar exits the silver-chunk of car muscle,
Into her grandmother's laughter and thin arms.

What wonderful light the eyes in the forest must see,
How wonderful the air the lungs must breathe,
How beautiful the fruit gathered by reaching up,
Stretching, into a tree; what a wonderful Garden,
Smiling with the blessing of the Cardinal from Congo
In splendour and majesty before God's children.

The elephant car shines in the growing heat of day,
Its eyes will blind the night away, the weary night,
Where the eyes are wide, caught wide with the ride
That makes nothing of the city roads, knee high in water.
Has God sent the flood, knee high in garbage, Armageddon?
Floating shit from open city sewers sticking to skin.

City fevers, coughs and closed down clinics,
Cure me father for I have sinned, forgive me father
For I have sinned, close my eyes father, I want to see
Our Father, he who art in heaven with hallowed name,
He with power and glory, forgive my trespasses that
Led me into this city called Destruction.

On roads that bump and grind, she was born in the hedge,
Born a refugee from twenty-seven years of war, and
You want me to live more, in the dirt of the city,
Dreaming of bell towers, spires and the gateway
To the Celestial place, where the roads are smooth,
A gliding ride for the Cardinal's bolted pieces of silver car.

In her grandmother's village life is simple. The young men
Travel the Crow Road from Eden, to find work, to earn,
To send back to the village where elderly, women
And uneducated children break backs and strain muscles
In the fields, reaching high into the trees, sleeping on earth,
Dying from shivering bowels, no simple tablet cure here.

We cannot go near the Cardinal's car, must not touch
His roadworthy, fiery chariot polished and bright, like a
    diamond,
Like a blood diamond, earned from the art of loving,
Carved from the message of hope, forgiveness,
Washed with the washing of sins at a crossroads point.
But who will forgive thee, visiting Cardinal, for hypocrisy?

Death of a Lion

I am sat sheltering under tarpaulin,
Writing in the light of a hurricane lamp,
The light is flickering, a gasp, gulp-breath,
Choking, fading, trying not to die,
To keep the dimming shadows alive.

Rain is heavy, pounding and pooling
In the sagging roof above my head,
Dripping, dripping, dripping into
The blue plastic bucket on dampening earth,
And I am cold in this air, marrow-chilled.

My pen scratches: the innocent Lion,
He is dead, for crossing the ditch,
For coming too close to those who invade
His nature, his world, his space,
To capture his picture and place

In the memory of a holiday
Now shot through with guilt,
No dart for peace, a calming drug,
Just a bullet, the only solution,
Just in case our fears come alive.

And there are times when they do,
In the lurking, dimming shadows,
In the flicker of a life, that fright;
Not of death, but of disposal
And that shaken night-dream

Of how we may die without reason
Or cause, by straying in a mistaken place,
Leaving our pride ebbing in the mud,
Leaving our soul confused,
Blanking our survival's unexpected end.

The light in the lamp has gone,
Words unseen, unfound are washed
By the water leaking and dripping
Onto a page of ink blots, blots, blots
And marrow-chill fear no longer required.

England

"A face on which time makes but little impression."

The opening chapter of Thomas Hardy's *The Return of the Native* sums up the England I love. Although they are at different ends of the country, that description of the heath brings together all I feel about the North Yorkshire Moors.

Standing high on an isolated moor, waiting for the year to change before heading down to the sea, a bonfire and sky-watching, I discovered something circular about the Crow Road: it can take you back to where you have been, but with new eyes mysteriously implanted in your head.

England has been my land of rediscovery. As a teenager on Teesside, the world around me was on the cusp of closing down. Steel, shipbuilding and chemical industries gave me one ambition: to get out and see the world, to find fresh air and inhale. I left as an angry young man. The industry left as well.

I was born in Slough, upon which Betjeman had urged friendly bombs to fall. Between Slough and Middlesbrough, it seemed my starting point was the world's end. With my journey came my identity crisis; one of many, I suspect. In the north I had been teased and punched for sounding like a Cockney. In the south I found myself reviled for speaking like a Geordie. Prejudice seems to be linked to some kind of geographical embarrassment.

I was never satisfied. As a child I had wanted Lego, but my parents bought me Betta-Bilda. I wanted a Scalextric, but my first racing car set was made by Airfix. My first bike was a second-hand girls' and on one occasion my mother made me a shirt from my sister's old brownie uniform; dulled shapes where badges had been and buttons up the wrong side made it obvious. These things shape a mind, an attitude.

This dissatisfaction and desire to escape are linked to my childhood dreams of seeing Africa, sailing the South China Seas, fighting pirates, joining Sinbad on the Caspian, or riding like Taras Bulba across the Ukrainian Steppes. As a child I went through a phase of insisting on wearing Cossack-style pyjamas bought from a Grattan catalogue. Films and books informed me about these places, and I never doubted that one day I would see them. The seeds of not wanting to be in England were sown.

It was before I started traveling that I discovered poetry and found the courage to write, mainly in secret. The start came at the age of 17 when I felt the wow factor of Andrew Marvell's 'To a Coy Mistress'. Senses opened to my own raging hormones, helped by a Rigonda Bolshoi family stereo that could whack out Bob Dylan, I found voices that echoed my frustration and romanticism.

"My love she speaks like silence": Dylan's opening line to 'Love Minus Zero/No Limit'. This song remains my all-time favourite poem. It gave me the impetus to write down feelings as, in my tender age, I wooed my own Eustacia Vye. I had discovered a girl who was *the raw material of a divinity. On Olympus she would have done well with a little preparation. She had the passions and instincts which make a model goddess, that is, those which make not quite a model woman.*[2]

It all came to a kiss, and the start of my writing heartfelt poems. But, the guilt factor was in place. I could read poetry in English lessons at school, but write it? I was locked within the cultural repression of 'boys don't do that!' This book is probably about getting that chip off my shoulder, though it does not move freely.

> *"Had we but world enough, and time,*
> *This coyness, lady, were no crime."*

To my living room

The candles in the fireplace, carried by nine monks,
Are whispering stories in secret laughter
Within the bond of silence.

The whispers are glinting in the glass, swirling
The red wine slowly into an ellipse
Within the bounds of mystery.

There is sadness in the purple flowers
The eyes show it, as they lean
Within the vase of memory.

The room is gossiping, listen still
To the curtains swaying to sound
Within the chimney breast.

Mysticism around the light shade
Shields the taunts of misunderstanding
Within the realm of ignorance.

Dance to the music in another's head
Keep in step and dip to time
Within surrounding space.

The floor demands it.

Flying Kites

I watched you in late summers,
As the heat of the days faded
And picnic baskets were packed,
Deckchairs folded; modestly you
Changed out of damp costumes
Behind the slipping towels.

All those summers of watching
Modesty grow, you furtively
Watching to see who is catching
The glimpse of thigh or swelling breast;
Until that summer, the one
When you refused to even undress.

All those late summers of you
Running through dull light,
Fading on hard sand furrows
Ploughed by receding seas. Hard
On your feet through plastic sandals and
The ignored irritation of drying sand.

I watched you run, towing your kite
On a long wet string; it bounced,
Cartwheeled and crashed
And crashed again, missing the breeze.
Girl-stubborn, feet stomping you came
For help with another tightening tangle.

Then one summer, not the last,
The wind changed and your kite shimmered,
Crackled and flew in a long, low
Exciting circle of loops and swirls and
Dips and dives, soaring rapidly up
Before turning down with a crash – oh joy.

That summer the art came to stay
As you learnt to balance and trim
And when to tug and when to release.
Your tricks are with you, displaying
The mysteries of kite flying, on a headland
Late in the summer on a breezy day.

Summer and I watched you changing,
Quietly, confident in the world around you.
I watched your angled kite swooping,
Upwards to hang like a red kerchief
Against the blue, thin cloud-lined sky,
And mine, lower, more modest in descent.

Kerrie

Kerrie, she's putting herself back together,
Kerrie, she's looking into her mirrors.
Some are cracked.
Some distorted,
But she keeps looking, searching.
Kerrie's looking for a mirror that is true.

She told me how she stepped onto the Crow Road,
Tarmac black covering, white-line cat's eyes guiding.
But she stumbled, she fell onto the by-way,
The sleeping pill path to some glare of oblivion;
Frozen within the black glass, face to face with
The choice to turn back. She made her choice.

There is me, ashamed of my sex, my race;
Of ugly men with balled fists, bawling,
Punching, and a sharp and sudden kick
Sends Kerrie sprawling, broken jaw, broken rib.
Have you forgotten the origin, the original sin,
The shame and the pain where we started?

There is me, trying to make sense of it all,
Looking at the broken egg from which she crawled,
As I stand outside the mad-mirrored wall,
No king's horses, no king's men, only Kerrie
To put it all together again, and me drowned
In answers; stranded, half way up and half way down.

A man's fist pounds a flower into the ground.
A shaking man, with muscle, insecure
In power; out of control, drained and weeping,
Watering the ground so his weeds can grow.
She is a rose in a wheat field, all aglow
With hidden beauty, un-mirrored, wilting slow.

She is a dark child of Ciar, her nature has placed her
Back in repair; from kick, from punch, from intensive care,
Laughing with a scarecrow's hope, beyond her victim's
   stare.
Her back turned against the lightning-shivers across the
   mirror,
Her reflection broken, but she is not. She walks to the gate
To find a new fate, along the road, before too late.

To Wilfred Owen

Fear,
Nothing to fear
But fear itself,
So the cliché goes.
It is a slow panic that eats us.
Sandbags grow around our heads,
Weighing heavy on our isolation,
Piled high and over, like a play-tunnel
Created from cushions pulled off
The old sofa in the living room; ha,
Living room. Is it not the dying room?

Do you remember the peace?
Those slim years between the wars,
Distant wars, over seas, not channels.
Then we talked about futures, even
Happiness, options, shop shelves.
But the counter attack, anti-war, failed.
The lost romantics are buried in the trenches
Or too shell shocked, too stuttering,
And, above all, too much afraid of the fear,
Frozen by enemies tucked deep within,
Frozen to the spot, not best foot forward,

No best foot, and too loyal to run,
Too stunned to be one of Milligan's heroes,
Instead, gloriously strung out on the wire,
Losing face, never mind limbs, cut
To ribbons is the phrase, to ribbons,

Comrades entwined, twisting with each other,
These lovers have only each other
And the fear of a marriage proposed.
Take it like a man, it is your duty,
Pick up your honour with the bugle call,
To retreat. No, to charge
Ever onwards and over.

Order

Tributes: Leonard Cohen, Thomas Paine, William Shakespeare, Jonah

Boxes of ideas fill the warehouse of my mind.
Blurred stamps, marked out of time
Disguise their place of origin,
Display their misplaced rhyme
Beaten out on a homemade drum.

Corset-maker ideals persist, but the stays
They are not so tightly pulled, nor notions
Squeezed into whalebone; with age,
Time inside the whale has been spent,
With cheerfulness breaking through

From the sea to land where the back bends
To gardening, to binding up
Those dangling apricots of disorder
And pruning back the thorns that snag
To burn them in some misty November.

Thoughts, grown like mustard seeds
On damp blotting paper on a kitchen sill,
And snipped with scissors to serve;
Son, here is my harvest, worried
By dithering unoriginal brainwaves.

The warehouse shelves, spring-cleaned
And boxed in order: philosophies on the right,
Emotions on the left, and somewhere
In the middle, potatoes wrapped in newspaper
For baking conclusions.

Fuck the middle classes

I am a man
Stepping back into his eggshell

In my hands
I carry plaster and a bag of broken shell

I am crouching
Holding them preciously close

I am clinging
Close to my past and the comfort it brings

I am swimming
Inside myself from the culture that is mass and not for me

I am listening
Hand cupped to my ear to catch a primal scream

I am listening
Forced to, hand against the tribal scream

I am a man
stepping back into his eggshell

I am furtive
By day seeking distance through electronic connection

I am watching
One eye blinking as I re-plaster my jigsaw shell

I am precise
Lining up the edges so they perfectly fit

I am meticulous
Careful for the plaster not to spill or smear

I am thinking
Leaving a watch-hole to securely watch others through

I am cunning
A secret hole for my electronic connection

I am hoarding
squirreling my past in a space of constant time

I am active
Building my time-less dome

I spy with my little eye
A youth cracking his shell open
He carries his pieces with him
To the disco of mass culture
To the magazine stand of dreams
To the thumping of the drum machine
To the swooshing of the tube
To the red wine shelf of a supermarket
To the frozen chicken store
To the plastic McDonalds
To the Spanish beach
To Old Trafford
To outside the Porsche garage
To the lawn mower
To the photo-exhibition
To digital Polaroid

To Microsoft Windows
To the bride of war and peace
To the protest in the park
To a fuck in the dark
To the election
To the mortgage broker
The candlestick maker
To Uncle Joe
To the man who went to mow
To the bank manager
To church
To the alternative church
To the bride in the lurch
To the Human Zoo
To the Beatles and the Stones
To the queens on their thrones
To the library of discontent
To the encyclopaedia of refugees
To the old woman's swollen knees
To the key of the door
To linoleum-covered floor
To the dinosaur
To Bob Dylan for an explanation
To the doctor for examination
To the forest for plantation
To the sex shop for elation
To the fairground for vibration
To poetic masturbation
To the duty of the To Do
For the day when he steps back
As a man,
Stepping back into his eggshell.

Ukraine

The collapse of the Soviet Union swept away certainty. Overnight, people found themselves catapulted into a free market and overtly corrupt world. The Orange Revolution followed some fifteen years later. It was meant to bring openness and democracy.

Somewhere within all this, poetry was on the rollercoaster ride, with its ups, downs, dips and dives. Somewhere in all this the new Ukraine was having its identity crisis, as it moved from part of a powerful empire to an independent stand-alone state buffering Europe and Russia; a route for gas and oil, a vast agricultural resource damaged by Chernobyl, a home to Russia's nuclear fleet, under-invested grimy industries and poor infrastructures.

Somewhere within all this, simplistic arguments over nationalism, Russian loyalties and European dreams – stirred by corrupt political shenanigans – were ping-ponging between Eastern and Western Ukraine. Somewhere within all this, poets were wrangling over free verse or rhyming couplets, social conscience versus aesthetics of poetry, creating national identity or just telling it like it is. By 2012 poetry found a new shape and turned into a form of verbal jazz.

In spring Donbas disappears in the fog, and the sun hides behind
*   heaps of earth.*
So you need to know where you're going,
you need to know the man who can make the arrangements.[3]

The words of Eastern Ukrainian poet Serhiy Zhadan, whose work was summarised by a local critic as follows: 'His prose is so poetic, his free verse so prosaic.'[4] Poetry is booming in Ukraine and poet Oksana Zabuzhko believes it's more 'vivid and animated' since 2004, the time of the Orange Revolution.[5] That mass outpouring failed, and energy for change has been spent. Perhaps poetry keeps voices alive, although arguments over use of Russian or Ukrainian language continue to rage.

Post-1990, nationalists were trying to ignore Ukraine's Soviet link, and wrapped the nation's identity in folklore and Taras Shevchenko. In doing so, they created an identity crisis with images of false freedom and denial. Poetry has been caught up in this.

'There is perhaps no other poetry in the world that is quite so oriented towards the past. There's a good reason for this. No other poetry is seeking justifications for its people's right to exist in quite the same way,' wrote poet-turned-political analyst, Mykola Ryabchuk, in 1989.[6]

Between 1989 and 1996 there were the avant-garde artists, The Stanislav Phenomenon, grouped around the Western Ukrainian town of Ivano-Frankivsk. They were post-modernist, exploring new identity, the homeland, and amongst them were the likes of Halyna Petrosanyak:

And not removing the garb of a Dominican nun,
Knowing well what and for what you're changing,
To set off on the road intending not to return,
Surprising those who didn't think the word 'homeland' has
Such an inconceivable dimension[7]

I acknowledge the directional search; and toast the new poets of Ukraine. I am pleased they are part of a place that since 1996 has been my second home, where – because of the communal joy that underpins poetry – I found an even greater confidence to write, free of cultural barriers. Ukraine's barriers lie elsewhere, within the continuing socially- and politically-manufactured conflict of identity, missing the point that so much is already shared.

Maybe the success of Ukraine's leading modern poets is their knowledge that *the man who can make the arrangements* still has a role to play. That underbelly of corruption is inspirational.

The Rehearsal inside a Kyiv church

Above umbrellas of chestnut trees
Domes burn gold and glint the eye
To turn heads away from the place
Where teardrops fall.

Through the heat, through the haze
The sound of running water breaks
Beyond the bridge of solid state
Old people stand, sob and shake.

(Victims past,
Victims still
Of capitalist fears
Of communist hates)

Beneath the dome,
Beneath the cross,
Musicians gather to rehearse
Before the next curtain call.
And from the chaos of the notes,
The crash, the grind, the fates,
That tuning brings,
Comes the blend of sound,
Drones and trills,
Dips, soars, as
Shostakovich cups his hands
To catch tears that fall.

Amidst the music pillars
The orchestra of state draws its bow
Across the strings to hang the note
Shivering in the space below,
Around the cross,
Beneath the dome,
The solitary mournful note
Calls the tears to fall.

Andre's Wood

Deer tracks lead in nervous steps back to the undergrowth.
Urine-spray colours the deep snow pale yellow.
With deliberate step, the hunter's footprint compresses,
Heel first, then toe. But the forest is silent.

Breath mists in the cold air.
In the paling sunlight, low in the sky,
Eyes try to pierce the staggered, orderly trees.
From mysterious depths, we are watched.

Nothing stirs as we turn, heel to toe,
Treading the winter's path through the wood.
The air is cold and fresh and deeply drunk
Into the lungs, before blown by reddening cheeks.

But we are not the hunters, just the admirers
Of Andre's wood, which, like a tale from Narnia,
Appeared one day into our lives,
And like magic into his life, forty-three years ago.

A loop of ice twined like a vine to a branch,
Dripping clear drops into the thaw of the day,
And each drop a memory of the wood that
Runs and stretches, breaking only for fire and wind.

History melts and mulches around the roots,
Signed by rub of antler on bark.
Each howl of some distant hungry wolf, or
A bear's rough growl, heralds another season.

And the seasons run into one. Even before
It became Andre's wood, it had a dream-life
Where patriots hid in the snow and fought
Bitterly against strange invaders and cold.

This passing spirit sanctum where all weaves untouched
Around the trees pillaring earth and sky,
Each mute witness to cruel killing, kind living, giving
Undecided sanctuary to the stalker and the stalked.

Neutral to the senses, events unfolding,
Like the day Andre walked with his love
Between the pines, or, marked and mapped
The trees for good economic usage.

There, as part of the system, yet
Never tamed, not truly, just managed,
So pines could grow taller and fall
Louder, and stronger. Man and nature

Forces for the common good,
Bark and sap and blood and bones.
The wood snap of twig and fall of leaf
Spiral history's roll into sawdust.

Reborn

Outside,
    Muted thrashing, shouting,
    Echoing hollow sounds
    That ring around the edges.
    Inside,
    Embryonic stillness embraces
    The kiss of a turning point
    Between life and death.
    Hands
    Above the water
    In sinuous spiral, waving,
    Even clutching, slowly clenching.
    Body
    Below the surface
    Sensing the new water-world
    Where dreams weave in refracted light
    Until
    Hands grab, hook,
    Haul you like a fish
    Into the rough bottom of a boat.
    Reborn,
    Out of time and place,
    You breathe the air
    But your soul swims with dreams and fishes.

Blue Eyes

Swim down deep into the river
Where fishes and dreams lazily glide
And glancing sunlight filters through
To carry the alluring sensuous scent
That pricks the soul of memories
And adds sweet spice to something new.
So dance in spirals
                              until,
With a final push,
                              you
Break the membrane
               of the water
                              and gasp and gulp
Air swollen by the freshness
               of blue-eyed flowers and grass.
With heavy boughs bowing down
So petals kiss the tension between water and air,
The jewel of this new-found paradise sits
Sending senses chasing bees around the blooms
To revere the beauty of
               A pale bud's perfect form.
And in a moment stirred
By the flash of a kingfisher's wings,
The air is captured by the petals' breath,
Freezing the hummingbirds' joy,
As homage is paid with a feast
Of crisp green apples washed in dew.
Welcome the unfolding nakedness
Of an angel with clear blue eyes

That release the boundary
                    of the skies.
And as stillness returns deep in the place
Where fishes and dreams glide,
A mirrored figure takes her chance
                        and flies.

Upon Ivana Kupala

Have I found you, my red flower,
My Chervona Ruta, has your yellow
Faded with the sun and been absorbed
By the fullest moon, leaving you
Naked in my midsummer night's dream?

I followed you into the density
Of the tangled wood, and watched
As, with fern-flowered princesses,
You weaved green stems into crowns.

Along the verge, hidden behind the hedges
Of that pot-holed road from Eden, Love
Was surely camped, waiting for her ambush,
Waiting to be found, after careless loss.

For you I wait, and watch you launch
Your flaming wreath and hope to catch it,
As I bathe under the waterfall of purity,
To wash away my beguiling sin of lust.

As the peal of church bells roll
Across the tops of trees, dispelling
Witches and devils from hiding places
Behind twigs and deadened leaves

That feed the leaping fire, whose stories
Glint in the glass of the cursing goblet,
Where your lips kiss, where mine do touch
And speak of Chernabog's return upon Korochun.

And in our time of love and coupling
Ancestors we will become, and
From the clouds behind the moon
Watch our sons and daughters swoon.

Love may conquer darkness, as
Darkness may embed love,
But I will seek with you to triumph
Until Koliada calls us into her light.

And so from the night, from the night
Of midsummer, let us hold hands and run
Down the pot-holed road from Eden,
Into the cycle of the setting sun.

A Friday cigarette and coffee in an Odessa café

Showtime music moonlights across the café room,
Crescendo kiss time

People sip into each other's eyes – turned bright at
The first taste

Pace change, and the flappers start their jive, hip-wiggle
Rock and roll is born

And as their starburst fades to soft French poetry, spoken
Over a piano

It is clear why Odessa is, at 8.45 in the morning,
A place of comedy.

Strangers Reunited

Lucky Strike and cold coffee memories
Unfold again across the square table
As the final click of the suitcase echoes,
On the day we met as friends;

Leaning against the bedroom wall,
Turning through the closing door,
Shoulder brushing the landing pictures,
Collar turned up against the cold.

We were enemies at war as the latch
Clunked shut behind, no more keys
To allow a step back indoors, only
The weight of a bag of clothes

Wrapping CDs and the odd favourite book,
Knocking against a painful knee, that walk
To the desperate café, to call a friend,
To find some laboured bed settee.

And then I took the road, and the road
Led me to skies and stranger lands,
And then a stranger, born to die
Until newly known again;

And so we are introduced as friends:
You say 'I knew him back then',
In the ragamuffin years of holes
And long coat pockets with lost keys.

That Friday-night knock upon your door;
You bought the drinks when a lonely coin
Was thrown into love's begging cup
And rattled heads-up before spinning tails.

Under a thin quilt, before a three-bar fire,
Orange-glowing, those years when strangers
Grew to know each other, before the lies,
Before growing again as strangers.

So we meet for coffee, circling
The square table, finding a seat,
And talk of the years in between,
Talking pictures, becoming friends.

Russia

'Blok belonged to pre-October literature, but he overcame this, and entered into the sphere of October when he wrote *The Twelve*. That is why he will occupy a special place in the history of Russian literature.'[8] So wrote Leon Trotsky about Alexander Blok, whose *Verses to a Beautiful Lady* (1904) are said, disputably so, to have launched the Silver Age of Russian poetry.

The poetic development in the twenty-year period that followed brought together a group of names that electrified literature, more so because they wrote in the period coinciding with the birth pangs of the Soviet Union. And then they struggled with the Soviet Union, culminating in Anna Akhmatova's *Requiem*, a shout that represented a million voices. She wrote, against Stalinist terror:

Seventeen months I've pleaded
for you to come home.
Flung myself at the hangman's feet.
My terror, oh my son.
And I can't understand.
Now all is eternal confusion.
Who is beast, and who is man?
How long till execution?[9]

In my younger years, many people tried to get me to join the Communist Party. I was always tempted, always felt like I was not true to the left by being outside of it. Those I knew and respected (still respect) like Nina Hibbin, a journalist, travel writer and film critic, were always true to the ideal. But I could never make that final step. I had studied the road to 1917 and the Soviet period; it had left a deep mark on me, adding to my fascination for the region, for Russia and a desire to see it. But I could not trust the abused ideal of Communism.

I have travelled broadly across the Russian Federation, along the Volga, Tatarstan, the Urals, and Moscow. I have visited most of the States that were part of the Soviet Union: Ukraine, Georgia, Tajikistan, Uzbekistan, and Azerbaijan. I have sensed their discomfort with the past and the anger at its result.

And I discovered beauty in the poetry. Ravil Bukharaev, who died in 2012, was a writer and poet who specialised in Islam in Russia, as well as in his native Tartarstan. His work is testament to the diversity of this landmass that covers such a large chunk of the globe. Inside his poems you can feel the hot wind blowing off the Gobi, and sink in the redness of the sky.

Suddenly
the Beautiful Beast said: there is no death but a cycle.
All that is real is equal and related;
all that is real is a part of me.

'The Beautiful Beast', he wrote, *is the incarnation, in the spirit of the Altaic epic tradition, of the wisdom and love of Mother Nature.*[10]

At the other end of Russia, St Petersburg – birthplace of the Silver Age, home to great composers, designers, writers, dancers – fascinates me. I get lost in the artistic and historical vibrancy of this city built on blood and bones and swamps, as did the great man who is credited with giving Russia its language. The streets of the city gave Pushkin inspiration:

If I walk the noisy streets,
Or enter a many thronged church,
Or sit among the wild young generation,
I give way to my thoughts.[11]

St Petersburg

Bright white blears the eyes,
Face cold, body hot – wrapped
Against the chill slices of breeze,
Blown from the breaking iced Neva,
Along the lines of Kanal Griboedova.
Here upon the apex of this footbridge,
Pressed against the hoar-frosted rails,
Half shaded by yellow lamps,
Our breath mingles in the crisp air
And marries our past and present.

The crowd sweating vodka,
Laughter,
Moves on silence,
Passes around us
With the occasional jostle.

In this timeless light, in this déjà vu moment,
Who can talk about a future when overawed
By the gilded Church of Spilled Blood,
By the tiers of ceramic saints
Staring down from their kokoshniki gables?
Still Diaghilev merged and blended
Our cultural breath, our differing tastes
And sets out ballet against this backcloth
Of then, now; history seen,
But the invisible is frozen from the eye,
But, again but, the imagination can roam
Disguised as a nose that knows
Where the breeze is blowing
Along Fontanka, down by the Moyka,
To be requiemed by Akhmatova.

The crowd sweating vodka,
Laughter,
Moves on silence,
Passes around us
With the occasional jostle.

Did Rastrelli design you too?
In every angle, your cheeks are shaped,
Your eyes the blue of St Petersburg,
Your classic flow of simple line
Drawn around and down your side,
A bride-lover to this dance, to this man.
A master of his victory.
A slave to his weakness.
A creator who fears failure.
A Myshkin compassion in his genes.
Rasputin incarnate treads these streets,
Even today, I heard his shadow-steps
Sweeping by, a chant, a whish of robes,
Stilled in the palace gate, pressing
Hard against cold, wrought metal.

The crowd sweating vodka,
Laughter,
Moves on silence,
Passes around us
With the occasional jostle.

Time is lost in its own past
And built to the present
In a piecing of assumptive jigsaw,
The guesswork of creativity,

'Tomorrow' the missing piece.
And the clock has been restored,
This piece of England,
This golden pheasant and glorious owl,
But it only ticks and turns
When the time is right to turn it on.
Rimsky-Korsakov, Borodin, Mussorgsky
You tuned your Slavic ways, and turned it on.
Pushkin, you gave your words to Russia.
'Art for art's sake' became the by-word,
The sly word was formed: propaganda.

The crowd sweating vodka,
Laughter,
Moves on silence,
Passes around us
With the occasional jostle.

Time's separation, time's difference.
We are lost in the confused mixing
Of stale breath stirred with the present
To freeze the dream of love's tomorrow,
Today.
Bright white blears the eyes,
Here, upon the apex of this footbridge
In this timeless light, in this déjà vu moment
Still Diaghilev merges and blends
But, again but, the imagination can roam
And marries our past and present
Staring down from their kokoshniki gables.
But the invisible is frozen from the eye,
To be requiemed by Akhmatova,
Drawn around and down your side.

The crowd sweating vodka,
Laughter,
Moves on silence,
Passes around us
With the occasional jostle.

Blood and bones have been the footprint
That brings me to this bridge,
To this half-shadow, amber streetlight,
To this cold moment, this shiver
That shows how grand dreams are built.
But, again but, the imagination can roam
Disguised as a nose that knows
Where the breeze is blowing
Along Fontanka, down by the Moyka,
To be requiemed by Akhmatova.

The crowd sweating vodka,
Laughter,
Moves on silence,
Passes around us
With the occasional jostle.

Tsarskoe Selo

Hidden memories are stirred and fired
By the simmering glow, chambered deep
Within the ancient mystic of amber.

You are found everywhere, at every turn
Of ankle and footstep old and new
Where the eyes rest on a painting, or
In playful statues' furtive glances, or
Skipping dance...

There!
There the hint of your hovering ghost,
Along the precise cheek-line of a masterpiece
Or cupped within the beckoning breast
Carved warm from the coldest of white marble.

The fawns and faeries bow, and silently laugh
As their playful spirits trip and turn you
Along the winding paths of Tsarskoe Selo,
Handing you from arm to arm to mouth
In a teasing, magical torment of moments.

Breathless I stand, eyes tracing the lips,
The shoulder – arm curving to delicate fingers –
Of the maiden cast into her dream, unstirred
By the broken jar and the spilt milk.
I cannot separate my eyes from this world,

Nor stop desiring the cream of experience,
Blurring me, you, us who gingerly hop, skip
And jump between the banks, the bridges,
The solid, golden swirl of an amber room,
Into the imagination.

Friendly Environment

The leaves in the trees
Rustled like charms
In the breeze

That warming sun
Dappled the broken
Path with shade

Walking you by
Lazy games
Being played

Eating ice cream
At Lenin's feet
On the parade

The environment
Is friendly this day
In Yekaterinburg

That is apart from the
Newspaper reports:
Please, don't look up

There is a hole
In the ozone layer,
The size of Texas

Exposing an area
East of the Urals
Above our heads

A Natural Spring Tapped Behind a Wall

A mid-day heat calmed only by shadows
From thin-boned trees with curled leaves
And shade from some angled building –
I pass across uneven cobbles, tasting hot air
In the dryness of my throat; my cracked lips
Desire a kiss of soothing coolness.
The stone set into the wall looks solid with age
And the brass tap pokes out, green in its stem.
The handle is tight, needing a twist of force.
From the nozzle I watch the bubble's expansion;
Slow, slow it starts to grow, as a grape,
Taut tension of its skin holding it there,
A tremble, a slight tremor and a refractive
Light of yellow and blue that draws the eye
Into some hypnotic state of waiting, watching
For the drip to fall, almost beckoning the tongue
To stretch out, head bent up, to suck it away.
And suddenly it drops and another appears
As a desperate hand turns the tap and
From deep within the hillside,
An age of water falls.

The Balkans

That the snow grows whiter
After a crow has flown over it
– Charles Simic[12]

Culture and politics makes us Europeans sharing geographical space a diverse group, but perhaps the force that divides us between East and West is Slavic soul. Western Europeans often liken it to some form of mass depression, once kept hidden behind that rusted Iron Curtain. It is, however, a lot more complex and vital than such a simple dismissal. Defining it is almost impossible, like the elephant: you cannot describe it in one sentence, but you know one when you see it.

'SlavicPatriot' – a pseudonym for a mysterious person who feeds YouTube – defined Slavic Soul: 'She is deep, mysterious, romantic, warm, at once wild, mad, melancholy, pure, honest, spontaneous, and sometimes naïve.'[13] The definition goes on to point to her black-and-white nature, which makes it hard to find compromise and change, but also acknowledges the high moral standard embedded within. St George, equally at home in British and Slavic culture, ride on! Even SlavicPatriot is missing one vitally important element: the ingredients for Slavic Soul are common. It is the magic mixing of those ingredients that creates the Slavic texture.

I stayed in Sarajevo and toured Bosnia, Banja Luka and parts of Croatia in 1997. I lived in Belgrade for more than two years from 2000, making regular return visits. I have enjoyed Montenegro and despaired in Kosovo. In 1980 my first honeymoon was spent in Yugoslavia, including a whole week (by mistake) in a nudist camp. My current wife is a Slav. I do not understand the nature, but I like it.

Poetry is perfect for the Slavic soul; but this raw vein of gold is not tapped enough.

In their paper 'A Survey of Bosnian, Croatian, and Serbian Poetry in English Translation in the U.S. and Canada,' Snezana Zabic and Paula Kamenish argue that if North American English-language culture chooses to ignore poetic practices in foreign languages, vital international influences on literature would be interrupted or lost.[14] There is much to lose.

Charles Simic viewed Yugoslavia's implosion from his US home. The Belgrade-born poet's work ploughs the deep traditional American roots of blues, jazz music and 'on the road' culture, but mixes in surreal ingredients drawn from violent Balkan history and traditions. Perhaps Simic comes closest to capturing the spirit of Slavic Soul and showing it to the west.

A lot of poems have, of course, emerged from the war; a war not just 'on Europe's doorstep', as many like to describe it. No, it was inside our living rooms. Izet Sarajlić wrote: *It's hard, of course | to write poems in the cellar | when mortars are exploding above your head | It's only harder not to write poems.*[15]

I am surprised by how few poems I wrote during my time in the Balkans. I managed to dig out some from Sarajevo, written as the ink was barely dry on the Dayton peace agreement; when the city's scars were on open display, shown through bombed-out buildings and street corners turned into graveyards. I think the dearth of poems is probably because I could never shape with words how a place so beautiful could turn on itself so easily. In some ways it continues to do so.

Only brooms
Know the devil
Still exists
– Charles Simic[16]

The Beauty of the Morning

The beauty of the morning
Is cast in the paleness
Of Sarajevo's unique sunlight.
Take this early walk,
Let eyes see beyond
The grimness of destruction
To the calmness of sniper-less hills.
In stillness they surround,
Unmoved and gazing down
City streets where people
No longer run, but stand still
Talk, smoke and even smile.
On this morning, when the air
Is crisped by the bite of winter,
Cleansed by the brush of ice,
And coldness giving life to lungs,
The beauty of the morning
Cups how good it feels
To feel.

The Beauty of the Morning (Revisited)

I turn my face into
The filtered paleness of light.
Exhaling smoke,
Balance and calmness finds me.
I remember with light
The softness and arcing curves
Of entwining moments,
Exploring the swell of hills,
The secrets of forests,
The strength of rivers,
And the beauty of the morning
Cups the goodness of feeling
Life moving.

My barrier,
My checkpoints,
They are down.
My calculations,
My gambles,
My debts to God,
Are consigned to a ledger.

I can be intimate again.

Light bulb viewed from a Sarajevo Street

Grey, grim towers line
The streets of Sarajevo.
Grim, grey faces move
Into and beyond ghostly visibility,
Followed by shadows
Unseen in their bleakness,
Unmoved by calling birds
Circling in the trees,
Preparing to fly
Like confused refugees
Bombed beyond surrender,
Into no surrender.
Beyond each bullet hole.
Beyond each crater.
Into and beyond
Makeshift crowded graveyards.
The footsteps of shadows
Remain two steps behind,
But in a tall, gutted tower
A light appears.

Mostar

The river runs clean
Through Mostar,
Rapid and green
Under remaining bridges
And places where
Bridges remain as shadows.
Fingers tap the coffee tables,
Suspicious eyes watch the divide
As, deep in the gorge, the river flows,
Trapped and channelled between its banks.
No stern lesson from God sweeps Mostar,
No flood or ark to send.
Just fingers tapping coffee tables
Eyes to watch division.
And still the river runs
Through Mostar.

Middle East

In 2008 I attended the packed, jammed, crowded funeral in Ramallah of Mahmoud Darwish, the Palestinian poet whose work became, according to the New York Times, a metaphor 'for the loss of Eden, for the sorrows of dispossession and exile, for the declining power of the Arab world in its dealings with the West.'[17]

Where
is my second road to the staircase of expanse? Where
is futility? Where is the road to the road?[18]

His poetry was powerful, but for me his most memorable words were captured as a memory on the eve of my 18th birthday. I did not know he had written them. They were spoken by Yasser Arafat and delivered to the United Nations General Assembly in November 1974:

I come bearing an olive branch in one hand, and the freedom fighter's gun in the other. Do not let the olive branch fall from my hand.[19]

My time in the West Bank, Israel, Jordan and Gaza brought me under Darwish's spell. A few days after his funeral I watched a film of one of his recitals delivered with sombre Arabic music, beamed onto a building wall in a crowded street. At a party near Ramallah, mournful, soulful recordings of his readings were played. Europeans cried without understanding why. The poetic voice of a generation had gone, but perhaps not lost.

He inspired me, perhaps more so because I witnessed his voice as a physical impact.

It was during regular trips to Yemen that I found a stream-of-consciousness coming to me, and suddenly I had written 'Beyond the Gates of Eden'. It came to me whilst seeing the vast desert and the volcanic plates of rock, whilst taking walks through the fish and vegetable markets, through old city streets, passing silversmiths and jewellers beckoning, spices smelling.

'The jingle-jangle-jingly sounds mix'. A first line later to be overtaken, but jingles and jangles were all around me. I could not stop writing. It was like a fixation that had to be gouged out of me. Something had impacted on my senses. I had chewed a little qat, the bitter bush that brings Yemen to a standstill in the afternoon, giving me a kind of amphetamine push. All these pictures came into words. Whatever else this poem might be, it is the result of an unprescribed experience.

I saw a lot of the country and its own juddering entry into the so-called Arab Spring. Yemen is an ancient land, one of the oldest civilisations, with spirits from historic times hanging in the ether. It is a corrupt land, an impoverished land. Today it is one of the poorest countries on the planet. In Roman times Yemen was known as Arabia Felix (Happy Arabia), famous for its frankincense and myrrh, and may well have supplied the three wise men heading for Bethlehem. In its modern setting, it is an unhappy place.

Poetry is an ancient art form for this region, often handed down in the oral tradition, celebrating some tribes and mocking others. It is believed that in some cases poetry battles were fought instead of going to war.

Anthropologist Naiwa Adra says that for centuries, oral poetry has offered a socially acceptable way for men and women to solve problems, manage conflicts, and communicate feelings of sorrow, happiness, and worry. 'There is a huge respect for [the spoken word] in Arab culture,' said Adra. 'If something is written, it's suspect; whereas if it's remembered, it's valued.'[20] The Syrian poet Nizar Qabbani wrote:

Light is more important than the lantern,
The poem more important than the notebook,
And the kiss more important than the lips.[21]

Beyond the Gates of Eden

*"For it is written that Abraham had two sons, one by the
bondwoman and one by the free woman." – Galatians 4:22*

*And one started the line of Northern Arabs and became a prophet
of Islam, the other fathered the Jews, and the line to Christianity.*

*And both fathered sons who inherited the sins of their fathers,
and made the bondwoman and the free woman one.*

Your eyes were caught in my headlights
As I was leaving Eden,
They were bright, filled with amazement,
And your smile an invitation
As the guards were busy changing
At the iron gates to the garden,
And suddenly, I was on the wrong side
Of paradise.

The jingle-jangle-jingly sounds mix
Qat calls in the overflowing streets,
Echoing through the night, the dawning,
That hangover in the bright morning,
That sleep in the afternoon vision.
The old market coming alive, circles,
Strung-out red skipping lights
Decorating the silver store, betraying
Your smiling hand upon mine, intention,
Squeezing a shiver, a shiver zipped
Inside a thought, a dream, a second split
And closed down, door barred. Stop.

Motorbikes jump and jerk, revving loud,
Weaving a knot around the knot,
Honk; pushing cars nudge refugees,
Knocking shoulders in the watching queues,
Jostling to buy tomatoes, Qat calls Qat calls
Yemeni cheese, Yemeni cheese, that squeeze
With a laugh, echoes in my mind,
Even the shiver is trembling through to
That zipped thought, that thought zipped.

And there I sit under Sirah Mountain.

Soon, the prophet says, that belching breath,
That fire, that explosion, that mighty bang
Will come, welcome, hand your sorrows out,
Before that path to forgiveness; too late
And too late it sang, the bell it rang,
Is it for you my coy mistress?

You look so beautiful this night.

The fire and the candlelight,
The fire, the fire, the fire, the fear
Is as bright as any candle.

Travelling beyond the ash
Into the lava rock of brown,
Of darkness, I need a light to step
Through the rigid back-plates of extinction,
Through the land of loss and waste;
Breathe in the scent of humidity,
That falls from soured grace,
To some other soured grace.

I listen to your story,
Wanting to take you into my heart;
But how could I be some bold deceiver,
A bold deceiver in the dance?
Let us dance,
Let us dance,
Let us dance
Along the road from Eden's gate
As sinners left naked, looking for cover,
Sinners one and two, but not quite together,
Not quite the same. Listen to my song,
Are my words not in vain? That day,
That day I paused in the lay-by,
Turned my headlights off,
Were you then the free woman?
Or did I make you the bondwoman,
When I tasted your given fruits
That moment the seed was planted?

That was the time of growth,
The beauty and the shame, caught
Within this salacious game. Hypocrites!
The makers of the laws joined
The makers of the punishments
And built high walls with all their books
Outside the Gates of Eden.
The women, threshold to the gate,
Turned blessings sour;
The blessing of the free woman,
The blessing of the bondwoman,
Turned sour like camels' milk
Cast from the jar, onto the stone,
To evaporate, a mother's milk,

And the spirit lives on,
Inside the sons that claim the purity,
And own the sins of their fathers,
Turning the steel of ploughshares
Into swords.
Pity poor immigrants,
Pity poor refugees,
On the road from Eden.

* * *

Will my father come today?
Will he bring a basket of apples?
Tonight will I sleep on this rough mat,
And will my mother be near me?

Will my father come,
With his basket of fruit,
Will I be able to sleep
And dream of tomorrow?
Will my sister play with me?
Can we drink from the well,
From the rain we welcomed
Each winter,
When we danced with a splash?
Will my father come?
Will he see me,
Pluck an apple from his basket
And throw it to me?
Will I wake on this mat
And know where I am?
Who I am?
Where I came from,
Where I am going?

* * *

Adam, you let her go, that perpetual demon.
Adam, you walked beyond the Gates with her,
Lost her and were left searching, who for?
Was it that middle wife, the one you left in horror,
The one you rejected, that perpetual virgin?
But the one who walks with you
Was not created from your head
> *God forbid a woman with pride*
Was not created from your eye
> *God forbid a woman who pries*
Was not created from your ear
> *God forbid a woman who hears too much*
Was not created from your mouth
> *God forbid a woman who talks too much*
Was not created from your heart
> *God forbid a woman who enjoys people*
Was not created from your hand
> *God forbid a woman who desires all things*
Was not created from your feet
> *God forbid a woman who is a gadabout*
She was created not from any of these parts,
And vengeful Adam – man of continuing sin –
Is she not a living being?
And is she not the one you take for granted
As you search for a woman who is
Proud to be with you,
Who is glad to hear your voice,
Who is pleased to talk with you,
Who seeks your pleasure,
Who desires your company,

Who walks with you
Through the gate and down the road
That leads from the Garden of Eden?
Oh vain Adam, whose line begat Abraham,
And the division of the world
And the double standard
And the covered part of creation.

* * *

Senses alive in the jingle-jangle-jingley
Aroma of the market place; crumpled note
To buy your fruit and taste it,
Taste it, by command of the market place
Where a man holds high the severed head
Of a serpent, a baptiser, a queen, and
A man revs hard his jumping machine
And flies to catch eyes
In his headlights.

The World Gone Crazy

Can you do sad eyes
Sitting with the hangman
Resting on your thighs
With a thousand-drum hum
And some hungry soul sighs,
Or do you smile and shun
The world that's gone crazy?

Can you pout
With a childish despair
Where split ends float
On loose hanging hair
With your dust covered coat
And streetwalker flair
Through the world gone crazy?

Can you frown deep furrows
Still showing that you care
Look for a tomorrow
That you want to share
Hold on to the sorrows
And show you don't care
In a world that's gone crazy?

Can you blow smoke rings
From a Cuban cigar
And cough out the things
Gathered from afar
And pull out bee stings
From the cup of your bra
Inside a world that's gone crazy?

Can you look in the snake eyes
Of some mystical sign
Weave a dream of the wise
On a simple white line,
Mind expanding with minimal size
Spilling the last drops of very red wine
Over a world that's gone crazy?

Beyond the Crazy World

"I have seen all the works that are done under the sun; and,
behold, all is vanity and vexation of spirit." – Ecclesiastes 1:14

Eve is in the living room
Sitting in her chair piled with cushions,
Biting apples.

Adam is in the garden
Hanging out the washing
And chasing blackbirds.

Cain and Abel are squabbling
Over broomsticks and horse-heads,
Playing war games.

Noah to the rescue in his ark
Picking up monkeys in the park,
God stands crying.

The church bells are ringing loud
Bringing all down to their knees,
Praying for the tears to stop.

Down by the river drowning in mud,
Down on the motorway driving hard,
Down where night-dreams are washed away,
Eve is standing in the half-light
Adam is looking for her tonight
Down by the gates to the park,

He takes her hand, slowly
They walk the route they know,
Stepping into the half-dark.

London is on fire,
The Thames overflows
The baker's burning loaves,
Fish shop chips are frying
In a deep heat pan
Like a virus
In a microchip plan.

Eve is drinking wine from the bottle,
Breaking bread with Desperate Dan
Screaming 'Jesus! Jesus was a man!'

The road from Eden is overflowing
With fast food sellers and crow trainers,
All looking for silver, preferring gold.

A man with cups is hoodwinking the queue,
Children lost, they don't know what to do
Apart from start a riot. Anyone got a light?

"For God shall bring every work into judgment, with every secret thing, whether it be good, or whether it be evil." – Ecclesiastes 12:14

The perfect escape from the fear of imperfection

It was not the story that weaved me inside,
Tying my strands and shaping them, no
It was the voice through grey hair, an
Unshaved voice, that carried clay out of man
Into the fairytale air.

Inside the voice the picture emerged,
Dented by thick accent, lined, pushed
And moulded by firm thumbs and fingers
That edged, smoothed, and sexually hovered
In the sensual realm.

Two lovers pulled from the clay,
Their entanglement smoothed to one,
The frustrated suitor running around,
Banging on an impenetrable door,
A fledgling bird flying free.

I watched the product of earth
Grow into the sky, nurtured
By an imagination, and sculpted
Into the space, spirited on a wheel
And breathed into life.

As his story unfolded I saw it;
That glimpse in a firelight,
Her ember eyes brightened, carried
Away on the twist of a shape,
Before dulled at story's end.

* * *

Inside this haven the wall is
A moon distance away, and here
We dance with the clay, but
We know the moon's shadow
Touches the edge of this world

And we know our shoes are stuck
Inside this clay, this solid trap,
Behind this sculpted line,
And we cannot dance away
Leaving our shoes behind.

Frozen statue moments, they spark
Our beauty inside, our walls,
Our escape into fantasy-realities,
And here we hide, we play, waiting
For the clay's crack and release.

* * *

I watched,
I listened as she shaped
The woman,
Motherly breasts, baby
Held secure in arms,
As she held the clay,
Cupped palms stabilizing
A statue that is not quite Madonna.

Raising shoulders, graceful windmill arms
Move as she nurtures and tends, encourages.
This woman's eyes want to give birth
And see birth given in her frustrated sharing.

I watched,
I listened as she shaped
The woman,
To motherly breasts, to child,
She declares the addition
Of a slight swell of stomach,
Adding that touch of imperfection
That others fear.

Shadow on a cliff wall in Wadi Rum

My shadow dances on the face of a mountain,
It moves to the heartbeat of a campfire.
My shadow is my past stretching before me
When the sun is at my back.
My shadow is my future; when long
It stretches to reach high points beyond me.
My shadow is small and still when I am standing
Still and in low light.
My shadow comes to life with a small candle
And dies in the dark.

And finally...

Epitaph: The Crow Road's End

The noise of the Crow Road fell into silence.
I stood stunned before the Gates of Gold.
I saw the bars, the locks, the empty key ring.
I knew he was watching my every move.
'Let me in Peter,
                Let me in,'
                                I cried.
                                                I cried.
I had bought four roses this soulful day.
A kerb-side seller took money from my purse.
I was on the avenue of fearful footstep.
I held her hand as she robbed me blind.
'Let me in Peter,
                Let me in,'
                                I cried.
                                                I cried.
The Padre asked me, he had to, he had to ask.
'Are you a Catholic?' He smiled when I said no.
'It does not matter,' he said. 'It does not matter.'
I made an excuse and put a heart on his plate.
'Let me in Peter,
                Let me in,'
                                I cried.
                                                I cried.

'I am sorry. I am sorry for all my wrongdoing.
I am sorry. I am sorry for all my weak sins.
I am sorry. I am sorry for the lies I told.
I am sorry. I am sorry for the stolen gold.
Let me in Peter,
                    Let me in,'
                              I cried.
                                        I cried.
The art of forgiveness cannot be practiced here.
His voice was thin. His voice was a toned despair.
Cataract eyes said *love and abuse walk side by side.*
'You walked,' he said, 'but kept your own gates closed.'
'Let me in Peter,
                    Let me in,'
                              I cried.
                                        I cried.
'I,' said Peter, turning upside down, pinned before eyes,
'Cannot help you now; see The Gates were never lies.
These gates were never shut as tight as your lids.
You do not have to be asked to pass this way. Or ask.'
'Let me in Peter,
                    Let me in,'
                              I cried.
                                        I cried.

And I looked through the gates, beyond the keys
Beyond the non-existence of the other side, He
Stood there arms open wide, pinned and crucified.
He looked at me and spoke: 'You who cries! Decide,
To let *me* in.
                    Let me in,'
                              He cried.
                                        He cried.

Endnotes / References

[1] Laurence, M. and Foster Stovel, N. (1976) *Heart of a Stranger*. University of Alberta, p.56.

[2] Hardy, T. (1937) *The Return of the Native*. Forgotten Books (2008), p.68.

[3] Zahan, S. (trans. Tkacz, V. and Phipps, W.). Poetry International Web (2011) *The Mushrooms of Donbas*. [online]

[4] Melnikov, R. and Tsaplin, Y. (2007) North-east south-west. *UFO Independent Journal of Philology*, 85

[5] Zabuzhko, O. and O'Callaghan, R. (2009) A Democratic Art: Poetry In The Ukraine. *Poetry Review*, 99 (1).

[6] Ryabchuk, M. (1989). (trans. Kaczmarsky, V., 2005). Poetry International Web. *"We'll die, not in Paris"*. [online]

[7] Petrosanyak, H. (2000). (trans. Naydan, M., 2000). Poetry International Web. [online]

[8] Trotsky, L. (1924). *Literature and Revolution*. (trans. Strunsky, R., 1925) [online]

[9] Akhmatova, A. (1940). *Requiem*. (trans. Kline, A.S., 2005) [online]

[10] Bukharayev, R. (trans. McKane, R.) (2001) Commentaries on Love 23: The Beautiful Beast. *Modern Poetry in Translation*, 17, p.67.

[11] Pushkin, A. (1829). (trans. Ledger, G.R., 2009) [online]

[12] Simic, C. (1975), 'Brooms', in Halpern, D. ed. (1975) *The American Poetry Anthology*. Avon Books

[13] SlavicPatriota (2012) *Slavic soul definition*. [video online]

[14] Kamenish, P. and Zabic, S. (2006) A Survey of Bosnian, Croatian, and Serbian Poetry in English Translation in the U.S. and Canada. *CLCWeb: Comparative Literature and Culture*, 8 (3).

[15] Sarajlić, I. (1994), 'A Theory of Maintaining Distance', *Sarajevo's War*.

[16] Simic, C. (1975) (see [12])

[17] Shatz, A. (2001) A Poet's Palestine as a Metaphor. *The New York Times*, [online] 22nd December.

[18] Darwish, M. (trans. Joudah, F.) (2007) *The Butterfly's Burden*. Copper Canyon Press.

[19] Al-bab.com (1974) *Arafat's gun-and-olive-branch speech to UN, 1974.*

[20] O'Connell, K. (2004) In Yemen, Fighting Illiteracy Through Poetry. *National Geographic*, [online] 27th January.

[21] Qabbani, N. (trans. Frangieh, B. and Brown, C.) (2003) *Light Is More Important Than The Lantern*. [online]